5-MINUTE Hockey STORIES

Meg Braithwaite

Illustrations by Nick Craine

Collins

5-Minute Hockey Stories
Text copyright © 2017 by HarperCollins Publishers Ltd.
Illustrations copyright © 2017 by Nick Craine.
All rights reserved.

Coin images © 2017 Royal Canadian Mint.
All rights reserved.

ZAMBONI and the configuration of the Zamboni® ice resurfacing machine
are registered trademarks of Frank J. Zamboni & Co., Inc.

Published by Collins, an imprint of HarperCollins Publishers Ltd

5-Minute Hockey Stories includes certain imagined elements in tales based on real events.

HarperCollins books may be purchased for educational, business,
or sales promotional use through our Special Markets Department.

HarperCollins Publishers Ltd
2 Bloor Street East, 20th Floor
Toronto, Ontario, Canada
M4W 1A8

www.harpercollins.ca

Library and Archives Canada Cataloguing in Publication
information is available upon request.

ISBN 978-1-44345-398-1

Printed and bound in China
RRD/SC 9 8 7 6 5 4 3 2 1

Contents

NIGHT SKATING

P.K.'s summer was long gone.
He had been in school for a month already.
But what P.K. was really excited about wasn't
school or Thanksgiving or holidays.
What P.K. was excited about was hockey.

He loved watching hockey on TV with his dad and his brothers and sisters. But what he liked most was playing hockey himself, skating around the rink with his stick and pretending he was one of the great players he saw on TV.

P.K.'s dad had been taking him skating ever since P.K. had learned to walk. P.K. loved skating so much that he wanted to go all the time. But now it was October and still too early for most of the outdoor rinks in the city to be ready.

Besides, P.K. sometimes had to wait until his father came home from work. And by that time, the skies were dark, the streetlights were on, and most other children his age were getting into their pajamas and brushing their teeth.

One night, P.K.'s dad realized there was one place that already had ice and would be open at any time of the day— or night. He bundled P.K. into the car with his skates and hockey stick.

3

P.K. sat in the dark car as his father drove through the city streets. They were heading downtown. The buildings were getting taller and taller. Their bright windows lit up the black sky.

Finally, his dad stopped the car. P.K. could see that in between all of the big buildings was an ice rink.

walked over to the ice. There were a few people skating around. P.K.'s dad told him they were standing in a place called Nathan Phillips Square, and the big, curving building behind them was Toronto's city hall.

It was an exciting place to be at night. Over the rink were three white arches, sparkling with lights. P.K. could see hot dog vendors with their carts on the sidewalks. They were packing up for the night, but the smell of hot dogs was still in the air.

P.K. sat on a stone bench while his dad tied up his skates. P.K. and his dad just sat, waiting for the other skaters to leave. Then they stepped out onto the ice.

Their skate blades cut into the ice as they skated around, all alone on the big rink. The red and white lights of the cars on the streets flashed around them. The moon glowed above them. They passed a puck back and forth, imagining they were hockey stars, playing to the cheers of huge crowds.

Before P.K. knew it, it was time to go home. He was hungry. "How about a slice of pizza?" said his dad as they unlaced their skates. P.K. grinned.

After that, every night when his dad came home from work, P.K. would ask to go skating. Sometimes his dad was tired. Sometimes he wanted to stay in his warm, cozy house.

Sometimes his father got home from work so late that P.K. was already asleep. But his dad knew that P.K. would be upset if he woke up in the morning and they hadn't been skating. So P.K.'s dad would wake him up, and they would head downtown in the dark night.

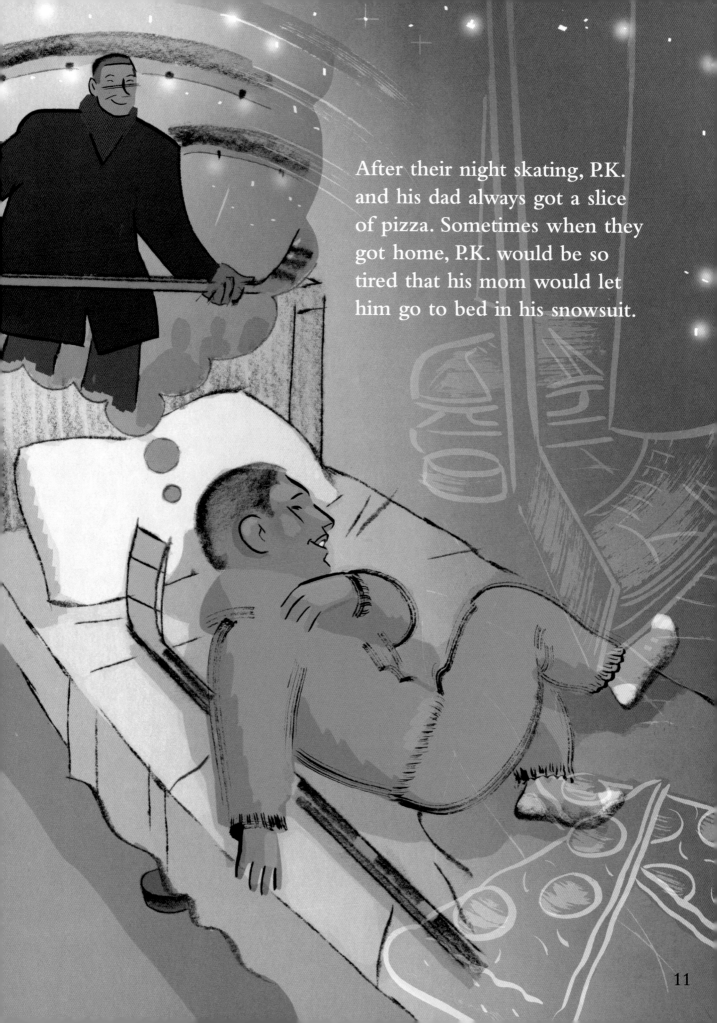

After their night skating, P.K. and his dad always got a slice of pizza. Sometimes when they got home, P.K. would be so tired that his mom would let him go to bed in his snowsuit.

11

P.K. kept skating, and he kept playing hockey, until one day, he stepped on the ice as an NHL defenceman. That was a special feeling.

But maybe not quite as special as those nights of skating in the dark, all alone with his father, on the big-city rink, the smell of hot dogs in the air and the city lights sparkling around him.

MAGIC IN THE ICE

When you watch a hockey team win a game,
who do you think made that happen?

Was it the goalie who stopped the shots?
Was it the players who scored the goals?
Was it the coach?

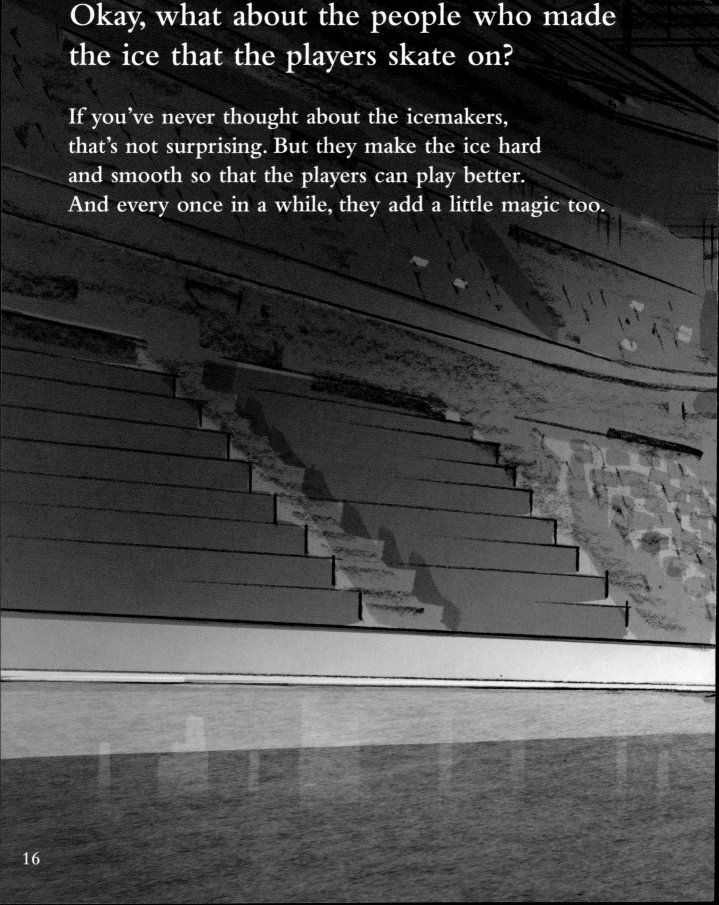

Okay, what about the people who made the ice that the players skate on?

If you've never thought about the icemakers,
that's not surprising. But they make the ice hard
and smooth so that the players can play better.
And every once in a while, they add a little magic too.

That's what Canadian Trent Evans
did when he made the ice rink
for the gold-medal hockey games
at the 2002 Olympics.

18

Men's and women's teams from all over the world were coming to play hockey in the Salt Lake City Olympic Games. Trent had been asked to help make the rinks.

He was excited. The rink he was working on would be used by both Canadian hockey teams—the women's and the men's. And they would be playing for the biggest prize of the Olympics—the gold medal. But Trent was also worried.

The women's team would be playing the United States. They had lost to the Americans at the last Olympic Games. And the men's team! They hadn't won a gold medal at the Olympics for fifty years.

Millions of Canadians would be watching the games in the arena and on TV, and every one of them wanted to see their teams get those gold medals. Trent knew that if the teams won, the whole country would be happy.

If they lost, well . . .

Trent started to work on the ice. After he put down the first few layers, he walked to the centre of the rink. Usually, there was a yellow dot painted at the bottom of the ice so that later the icemakers would know exactly where to put the centre faceoff circle.

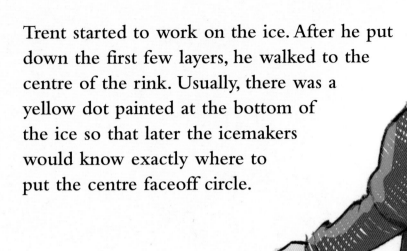

But when Trent looked down, he couldn't see anything there. He would have to add that dot now. There wasn't any paint around, but that wasn't going to be a problem. Trent already had a plan.

Trent wanted to help his teams. He knew that making perfect ice was the best way, but he also thought he might be able to make the ice special—and lucky —for the Canadians.

He dug in his pocket and took out a Canadian dime. He placed it in the middle of the ice, where the dot should have been. But when the next layer of ice was put down, Trent couldn't see the dime.

So he put his hand in his pocket again and pulled out a gold-coloured coin—a loonie.

He put it carefully over the dime and then added more water to the rink to make the last few layers of ice. Trent didn't want anyone else to find out about the loonie, but he thought it might help if the Canadian players knew. So he shared the secret with them.

Now he would just have to wait and see if it worked.

A day later, the women's hockey team had their game. The Canadians played well. But so did the Americans! In the final period, Canada was ahead by one goal, but the Americans kept shooting at the net. Try as they might, they just couldn't tie the game.

The Canadians won!

When the game ended, all the Canadian players were jumping around, laughing and smiling. Trent was on the ice too, clearing away equipment. Then he noticed three players skating over to the centre of the rink. They dropped to their knees and kissed the ice, right where the loonie was.

Trent was scared! What if the Americans wondered why they had done that? What if someone checked and saw the loonie? Trent would then have to take it out before the men played. He wanted to rush over and tell them to stop. But then the players skated away. Phew!

A few days later, it was the men's turn to play the American team. Trent noticed that the Canadian captain tapped his stick quickly on the ice on top of the loonie before the opening faceoff. Trent took a deep breath. Would the loonie bring luck a second time? Would the loonie help the Canadian men win the gold after fifty long years?

The Canadian players flew across the ice. The goalie stopped puck after puck. They were up one goal, then two, then three!

26

In the last few minutes of the game, the fans were so excited they started singing "O Canada."

Finally the buzzer went off. The Canadians had won! Trent was smiling. Now the men would get shiny gold medals, just like the women.

But Trent didn't have time to celebrate—not yet.

He didn't want anyone else finding the "lucky loonie." He didn't want anyone else taking it away.

As soon as the rink emptied—the players back in the locker room celebrating; the fans all leaving the arena and heading home—Trent walked across the ice. It no longer looked hard and smooth. It was scratched and scuffed, but Trent was proud of the ice he had made. And proud of the little bit of magic he had buried inside it. When he got to the centre of the rink, he kneeled down and began to dig for his coin.

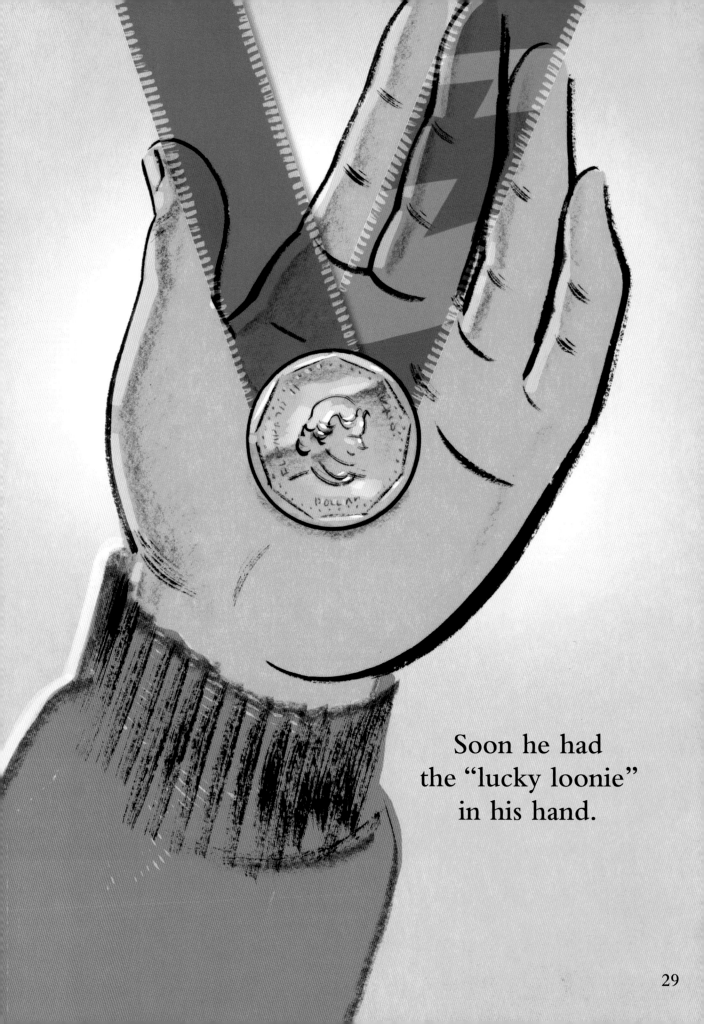

Soon he had
the "lucky loonie"
in his hand.

Don't you think it would be great to be the Stanley Cup? If you were the Stanley Cup, you'd be one of the most famous trophies in the world. You'd be loved by millions. You'd be right there in the rink, watching every NHL championship game. After the deciding game was over, the best players in the world would hold you over their heads and skate around the ice with you.

And then you'd travel all around the globe, spending a day at the home of each winning player! What could be more fun than hanging out with the best hockey players in the world?

Well, not so fast. Sure, the Stanley Cup is hockey's most adored trophy. But it's had some rough travels. And some crazy ones too.

Going home with the winning players hasn't always been so easy for the poor Stanley Cup. Detroit Red Wings player Red Kelly decided to sit his small baby inside the Cup. It would have made a cute picture— except nobody told the baby how important the Cup was, and the little guy peed in it.

Perhaps Carolina Hurricanes player Doug Weight didn't know this. The day he had the trophy, he made a huge ice cream sundae and then let his family eat it right out of the Cup. Another player drank soup out of it. One player gave his dog supper in the trophy; another let a horse eat from it.

But if you were the Cup, you would have faced real danger too. In 1962, at a victory celebration by the Toronto Maple Leafs, the Cup somehow got tossed into a bonfire! The Leafs players had to pay to repair the scorched trophy.

The Stanley Cup has also had some watery adventures. In 1991, Pittsburgh Penguin Phil Bourque jumped into Mario Lemieux's swimming pool with the trophy, and in 1993, Lord Stanley's Cup took a dip in the pool of Montreal Canadiens goalie Patrick Roy.

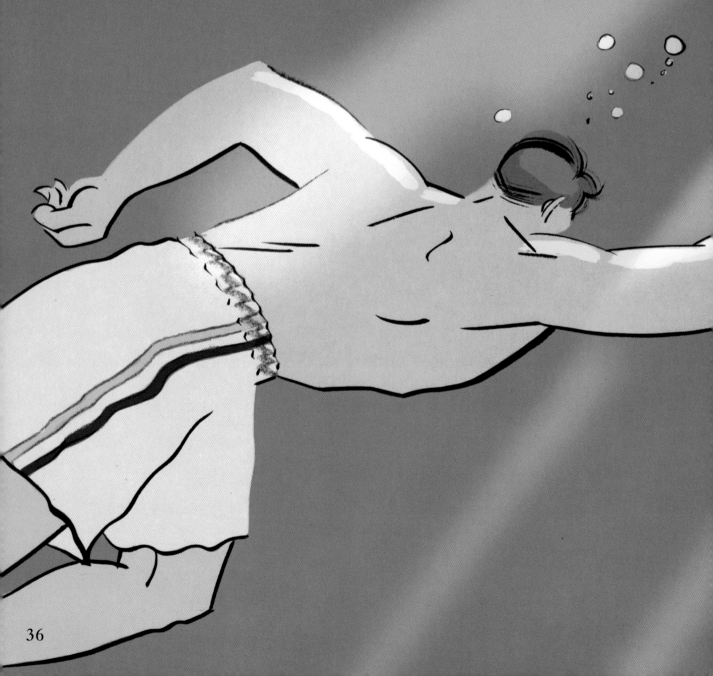

Clearly, the Stanley Cup has sometimes had a little too much attention! But it has also had too little. In the off-season of 1984, two Edmonton Oilers decided to take the Cup with them when they went out for the evening. But one of the players had a new car. He thought the big trophy might damage the leather seat. So he threw the Stanley Cup into the trunk. The players could hear the Cup banging and rattling around back there as they drove around town.

Worse yet, in 1924 Montreal Canadiens players put the Cup by the side of the road while they changed a flat tire on their car. Then the players took off, headed for a post-win celebration.

When they got to the party, they realized they had forgotten one of the most important guests.

They drove back, and there was the Stanley Cup, all alone, still sitting on the side of the road.

And in 1907, the Montreal Wanderers had their photo taken with the Cup and then forgot it at the home of the photographer.

When they finally went back a few weeks later, the photographer's mother had planted flowers in it.

So the poor Stanley Cup has had some interesting travels. But most of the time it gets treated well. If you were the Stanley Cup, you would even have hung out with soldiers. From 2007 to 2010, the Stanley Cup made four trips across the ocean to cheer up Canadian troops.

Two babies
have been
baptized in it.

It has been
taken mountain
climbing.

It has floated
in a canoe on
a fishing trip.

And it has been flown
up to the top of the
Rocky Mountains.

In fact, when Boston Bruins manager Milt Schmidt had the Cup at his home in 1970, he and his wife were so worried about how to keep it safe that at night they put it in an old baby crib they still had in their house.

When "the keeper of the Cup" takes the trophy to the championship game and then escorts it from player to player, he wears white gloves when picking it up and always sets it down on a clean, white cloth. And when it's finished its travels, it goes to the Hockey Hall of Fame, where millions of visitors come to admire it.

THE MASKED MAN

Did you know there was a time when NHL players didn't wear helmets and when goalies didn't wear masks? It's true!

It was pretty dangerous to battle the best players on the ice with nothing on your head to protect you from a flying elbow or a high stick, but imagine what it was like if you were a goaltender.

There you'd be, standing in the net, with players hitting rock-hard rubber pucks straight at you, while you had nothing on your head or over your face if the puck came in high or took a bounce. You wouldn't have had huge shoulder pads to protect you either.

Well, that's exactly the way it used to be for goalies a couple of generations ago.

And boy, did those goalies get banged up!

But a goalie by the name of Jacques Plante finally got fed up with all of that.

You see, by the time Plante had been playing professional hockey for about ten years, he had already broken many bones: his nose (four times), his cheekbone (twice—the right one, then the left), and he'd even fractured his skull.

Jacques wanted to find some way to protect his face. The problem was that the flimsy leather and plastic masks that goalies had tried before didn't do much good.

Then a guy who worked at a fibreglass company saw Jacques get hit in the forehead with a puck during a game. He offered to make Jacques a mask that might really help.

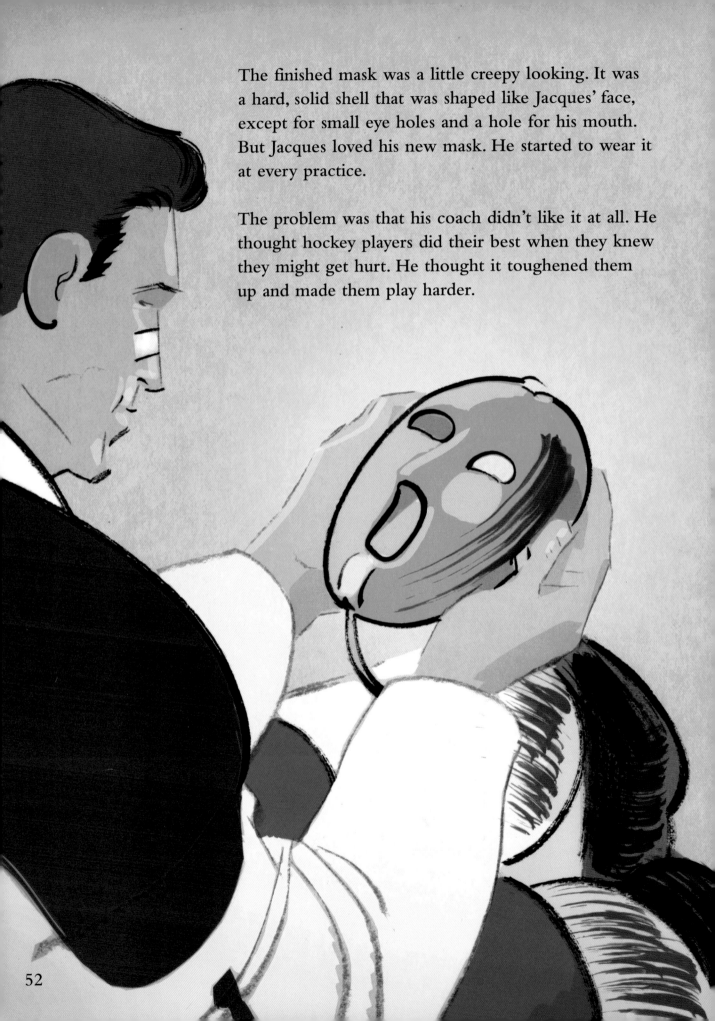

The finished mask was a little creepy looking. It was a hard, solid shell that was shaped like Jacques' face, except for small eye holes and a hole for his mouth. But Jacques loved his new mask. He started to wear it at every practice.

The problem was that his coach didn't like it at all. He thought hockey players did their best when they knew they might get hurt. He thought it toughened them up and made them play harder.

He thought the mask made Jacques look weak and afraid. The coach told Jacques he couldn't ever wear the mask in the real games. Jacques was frustrated, but he did as his coach said.

Then one night, during a game, one of the players on the other team took a hard shot on the net. It hit Jacques right in the face. It cut his face and broke his nose and one of his cheekbones. Jacques skated off the ice and went to the dressing room so a doctor could look at him.

In the locker room, the doctor set Jacques' nose and sewed up his cut with seven stitches. Then the coach came over. He expected Jacques to get back out on the ice so the game could start again. But Jacques had had enough.

In those days, the pro teams didn't have backup goalies. When a goalie left the ice, the game stopped, and everyone had to wait for him to return. "No," said Jacques. Then he told his coach he wouldn't go back out unless he could wear his mask. His coach was upset.

The minutes were ticking by. The players and fans were waiting for the game to start again. "Okay," the coach finally said. "You can wear the mask. But only until your cut heals up." After that, the coach said, Jacques would have to play without the mask again.

Jacques skated back onto the ice in his mask. The other players and the fans were shocked. They thought Jacques looked weird. They thought he looked wimpy.

But then something amazing happened. Jacques played so well that the Canadiens won that game. And the next. And the next. Jacques and his team went on to win eleven games in a row (making their winning streak eighteen games long). By then Jacques' cut had healed.

Lots of people were teasing Jacques about wearing the mask.

He didn't care. He wanted to keep wearing it. But he had made a deal with his coach. So in the next game, Jacques played without the mask. The Canadiens lost.

The coach wanted to win.
The team wanted to win.
The fans wanted to win!

So the coach let Jacques put
the mask back on for the
next game. The team started
to win again. That season,
the Canadiens skated away
with the Stanley Cup.

Although it took a while for goalies, players, and fans to accept the idea of the mask, within about ten years, almost all goalies were wearing some version of a face mask.

Today all players wear helmets, and goalies wear helmets and masks that are often painted and designed to look both cool and fierce. And we all have a goalie named Jacques to thank for that!

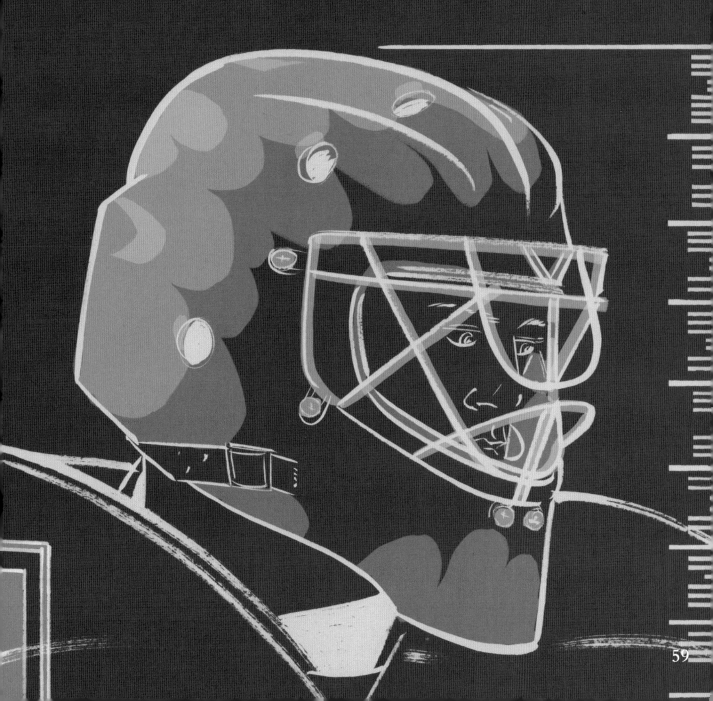

THE BEST FIRST GAME

Auston Matthews did not grow up in a place with ice and snow and plenty of hockey-loving folks. Instead, he grew up in the warm desert city of Scottsdale, Arizona, where most kids wanted to play football or baseball or basketball.

Yet right from the start it seemed that hockey was meant for Auston, and Auston was meant for hockey.

Auston's parents didn't know much about hockey, but they liked sports, so they started going to watch NHL hockey games. And they took two-year-old Auston with them. Auston liked that, but mostly because he loved watching the Zamboni machine drive around the rink.

Auston started playing hockey when he was five years old, and he also began to play baseball. At first, he was actually better with the bat than he was on skates.

But that didn't matter. Auston liked baseball. But he *loved* hockey.

And he was really good at it. In his junior years, Auston broke scoring records and was named the most valuable player at the World Junior Championship and the World Championship. In his last season before he could be drafted into the NHL, he played in Switzerland.

On the Swiss team, Auston scored so many goals and made so many assists that he won the "rising star" award. In fact, Auston was such a powerful forward that when the Toronto Maple Leafs were given the first pick in the NHL draft, they chose Auston.

So his Toronto Maple Leafs coach, his teammates, and the Leafs fans all expected a lot from him. Would he be able to live up to that? Auston knew he couldn't think too much about it. He just had to play the best he could and not worry.

Finally, it was the first game of the NHL season. Auston and the Toronto Maple Leafs were facing the Ottawa Senators in Ottawa. Would Auston live up to people's expectations now that he was in the pros?

Eight minutes into the game, an opportunity came Auston's way. The puck went behind the Ottawa net, but a teammate passed it back out front.

With two Senators in front of the crease, Auston skated across, got his stick on the puck, and with a flick of his wrist, shot it past the goalie. A goal!

Auston had scored a goal in his very first game in the NHL. His teammates slapped him on the back, and his parents were in the stands, clapping their hands and cheering.

But there was no more time to celebrate. The game started again, and the Senators took the puck into Toronto's end of the rink. In just three minutes, Ottawa tied the game and then scored again to move ahead of the Leafs.

ONE

A few minutes later, Auston managed to knock the puck out of the air, push it through the legs of an Ottawa player, steal it off the stick of another player, charge toward the net, and sneak the puck past the goalie.

His second goal!

The second period started in a tie, but the teams were on the ice for only a minute and a half when Auston found himself in front of the Senators' net with the puck on his stick once again. He took a quick shot and watched it whiz into the net.

His third goal!

TWO

A huge roar went up
from the crowd, and hats
were thrown onto the ice.

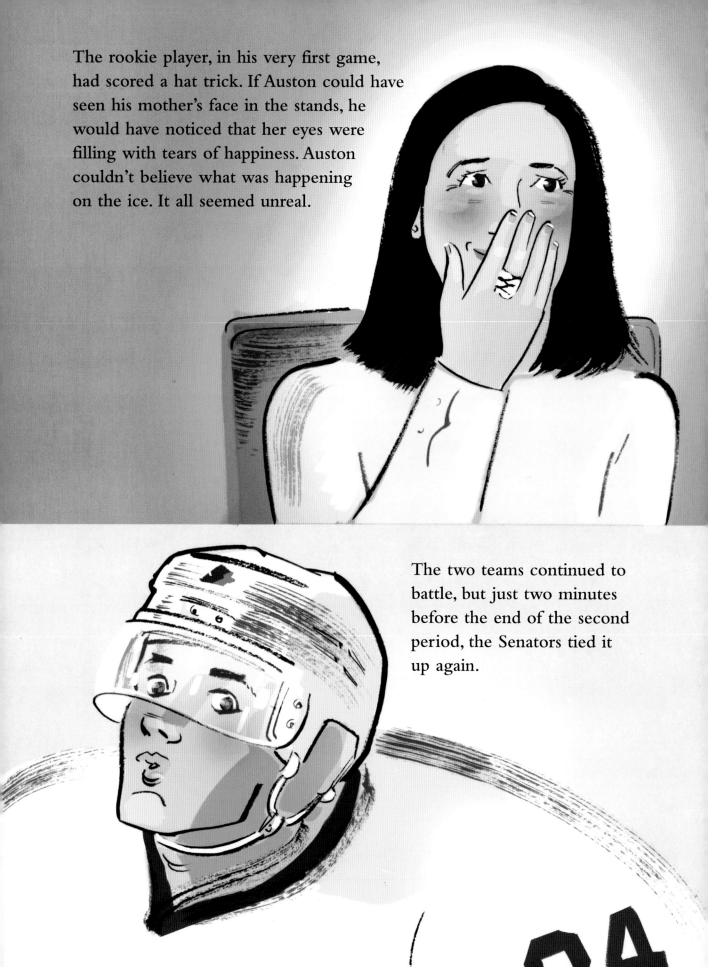

The rookie player, in his very first game, had scored a hat trick. If Auston could have seen his mother's face in the stands, he would have noticed that her eyes were filling with tears of happiness. Auston couldn't believe what was happening on the ice. It all seemed unreal.

The two teams continued to battle, but just two minutes before the end of the second period, the Senators tied it up again.

And then, something truly incredible happened. Just three seconds before the buzzer sounded to mark the end of the period, Auston got a pass from his teammate William Nylander. Auston was skating to the net as the puck flew toward him. If he missed, the puck would go past the net and into the corner of the rink. Instead, the perfect pass landed right on his blade, and Auston quickly snapped the puck past the goalie's stick and into the net.

His fourth goal!

Auston had just done something truly remarkable. In previous years, four other players had scored hat tricks in their NHL debuts, but no one had ever, ever scored four goals in his very first game.

After the third period, the score was tied 4–4. And, incredibly, all four Maple Leafs goals belonged to young Auston. In the overtime period, the Ottawa Senators scored to win the game.

Auston was disappointed that the Leafs hadn't won. But in his very first game in the NHL, he broke a record and played the best ever debut game in the history of his beloved sport.

Not bad for a boy from the desert!

WHAT'S IN A NUMBER?

Did you know that Wayne Gretzky is the only NHL player to ever wear the number 99? No one before him even had a number anywhere near that high. So how did he get that unusual number?

Well, Wayne Gretzky picked that number for a very special reason.

Growing up, Wayne was one of the kids who wanted to wear the same number as their favourite NHL player. For Wayne, that was "Mr. Hockey": Gordie Howe. Howe wore number 9 for the Detroit Red Wings. Gretzky asked for number 9 whenever he could—and usually he got it.

But when he started playing junior hockey in Ontario with Sault Ste. Marie, number 9 was already being used by another player.

He was disappointed but tried out a new number. And then a second number. But he didn't like playing with either of them on his back. He was missing number 9. That's when his coach made a helpful suggestion. Why not wear two 9s? (After all, if one 9 was good, two 9s might be even better, right?)

So Wayne had 99 stitched on his sweater—one of the many things that made the hockey star so instantly memorable.

Many NHL players pick numbers for very special reasons.

Sometimes players want to honour their own hockey heroes by wearing the same numbers. Jonathan Toews picked number 19 because that was the number of his childhood idol, Steve Yzerman.

Sometimes they pick the numbers their parents or family members wore. Alexander Ovechkin chose number 8 because that is the number his mother wore playing basketball for the Soviet Union in two Olympic Games.

And Auston Matthews has been wearing number 34 since he was a child because his grandfather wore that number when he played college basketball.

Sometimes players choose a number that represents a significant date or year in their lives—when they were born, or drafted, or moved from their home country. Sidney Crosby wanted 87 because he was born in 1987, in the 8th month (August) and on the 7th day.

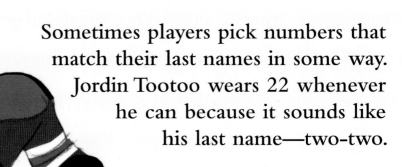

Sometimes players pick numbers that match their last names in some way. Jordin Tootoo wears 22 whenever he can because it sounds like his last name—two-two.

And years ago, a player named Eddie Shack chose 23 whenever he could because he thought it looked like his initials—ES—printed backwards.

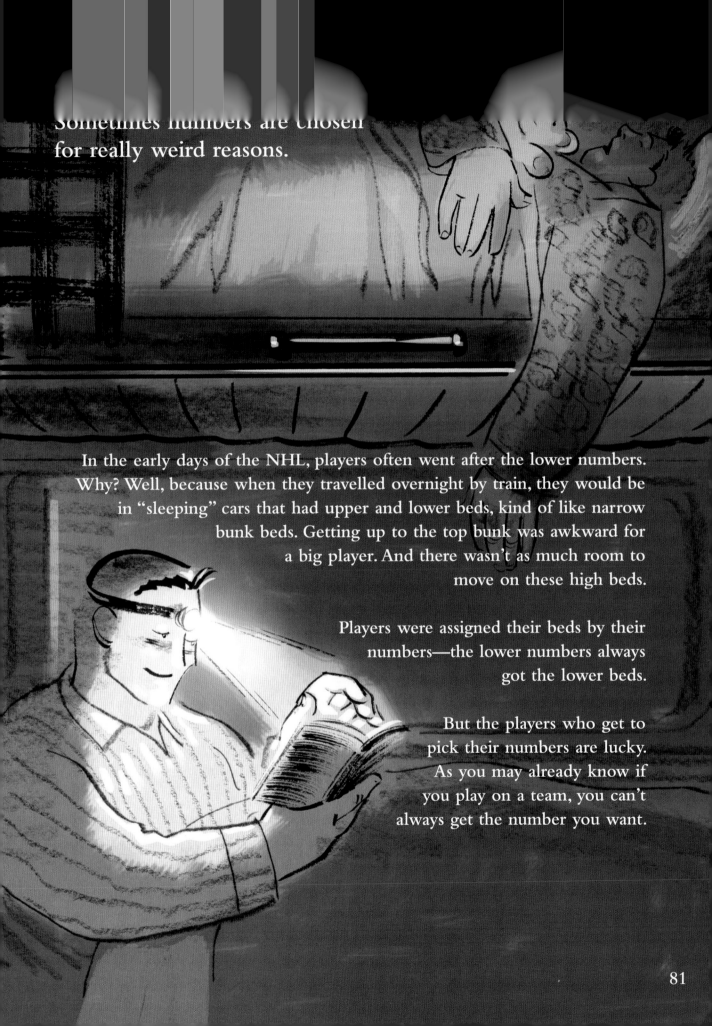

Sometimes numbers are chosen
for really weird reasons.

In the early days of the NHL, players often went after the lower numbers.
Why? Well, because when they travelled overnight by train, they would be
in "sleeping" cars that had upper and lower beds, kind of like narrow
bunk beds. Getting up to the top bunk was awkward for
a big player. And there wasn't as much room to
move on these high beds.

Players were assigned their beds by their
numbers—the lower numbers always
got the lower beds.

But the players who get to
pick their numbers are lucky.
As you may already know if
you play on a team, you can't
always get the number you want.

Some players, upon finding that the number they like isn't available, have some fun in order to wear their numbers—at least in a secret sort of way. They may reverse the numbers—so when John Tavares couldn't wear 19, he flipped the number around to make 91.

When 9 wasn't available to Russ Courtnall, he turned it upside down and wore a 6. (Mario Lemieux's 66 is 99 upside down—a nod to Wayne Gretzky.)

Or they may do a little addition: Pierre Larouche liked 10, but when he got to the Canadiens, Guy Lafleur was wearing that number. So Larouche chose 28 because 2 plus 8 equals 10.

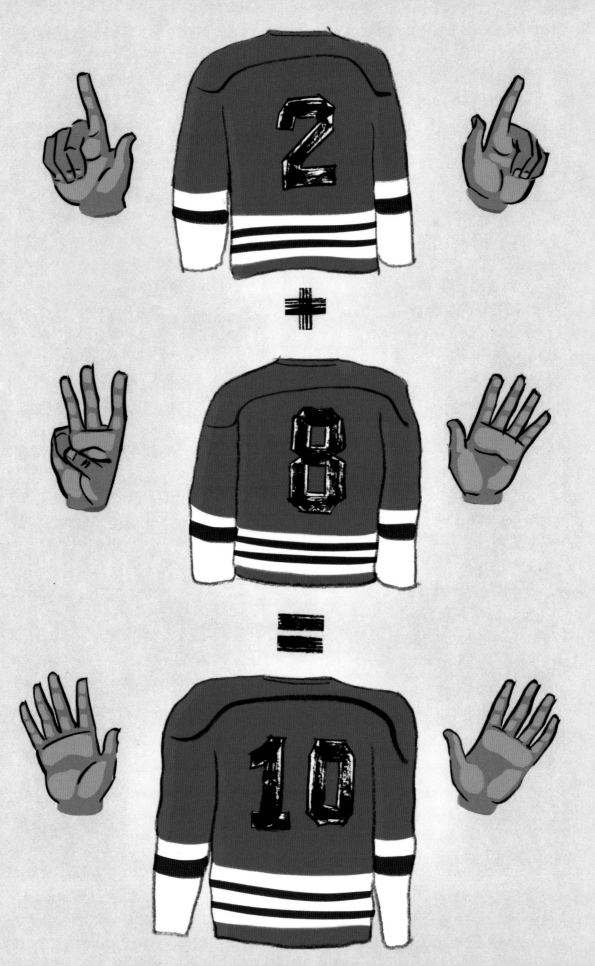

But there's one number that no one is ever going to be able to wear. And that's Wayne's number 99. After Gretzky retired, the NHL decided his number would be "retired" too. In other words, no NHL player could ever have it again.

That's how Wayne got to be the first and only player ever to wear the number 99 in the NHL.

AB'S
SECRET

Did you know that women and girls have been playing hockey for as long as men and boys have? In fact, the daughter of Lord Stanley, the fellow who donated the Stanley Cup, played hockey herself.

Back when your grandmothers were young, women were seldom seen playing ice hockey. Hockey was considered a sport for only men and boys. Most people thought girls didn't want to play—and that they couldn't. But in 1956 there was at least one little girl who didn't think hockey was only for boys.

Eight-year-old Abigail Hoffman loved to play hockey. She had learned to skate when she was three years old. Not long after that she started playing shinny—a game of hockey played just for fun—at a local outdoor rink with her two older brothers.

By the time Abby was in grade three, she wanted to play on an actual hockey team. When she asked her parents, they took her down to register for the Toronto Youth Hockey League.

When Abby and her parents arrived at the arena, they found it crowded with hundreds of little boys and their parents. There didn't seem to be any other girls there. That was because there weren't any girls' teams to play on.

Abby's parents thought there was nothing to do but go home. Abby, however, wasn't ready to give up. After all, she wasn't really looking for a girls-only team. She was just looking for a team. She didn't realize that girls weren't supposed to play on the boys' teams.

So Abby did what every other kid was doing. She walked over to the registration desk and gave the person there her name, her age, and her phone number.

Except she didn't say "Abby"—she said "Ab." Then Abby walked back through the crowd of boys to find her parents.

A couple of days later, Abby's mom got a phone call. Her son, "Ab," was on a team called the St. Catharines Tee Pees. Abby's mom knew that if she told the coach that Ab was a girl, he might say she couldn't play. So Abby's mom kept quiet. And Abby got ready to lace up her skates.

So what do you think happened when Abby hit the ice? Do you think Ab's teammates thought that "he" wasn't a boy? Do you think people watching the game thought there was something different about the way "Ab" played?

Do you think the coach suspected that the player named "Ab" might really be a player named "Abby"?

Of course not. The only thing everyone noticed was that Ab was a good hockey player. A really good hockey player.

Game after game, Abby showed up at the rink in her equipment and put on her skates with the other players in the locker room. Game after game, Abby checked opponents, stopped passes, and defended her goalie.

No one on her team knew Abby was a girl. But it was getting harder and harder to keep the secret. Her brothers couldn't help talking about their hockey-playing sister with their own teammates, and word was getting around. One day, one of the other parents winked at Abby's mom and said, "That boy of yours is quite the hockey player."

In fact, Abby was such a good player that she was chosen to join the league's all-star team.

That's when Abby's mom knew they couldn't fool people for much longer. After the first all-star game, the whole team would be going swimming to celebrate. Everyone would see that Abby was wearing a girls' swimsuit, not a boys'.

It was time to let people know that the terrific hockey player everyone knew as "Ab" was really named "Abigail." When Abby's parents told her coach, he couldn't believe it. Neither could a lot of people.

Back then, it was so surprising to people that a girl could play as well as a boy that Abby's story even made the newspapers, the radio, and the TV.

Once Ab's story got out, so many girls asked to play hockey that the league started a spring training camp just for them. Abby had proven that girls wanted to play hockey—and that they could play well!

After her season with the Tee Pees, Ab focused on swimming and track and field instead. Just as with hockey, she was really good at those sports.

She was so good at running, in fact, that as a young adult she won medals and broke records at the Pan American Games, the Commonwealth Games, and four Olympic Games!

Even though Abby chose to play other sports when she got older, women and girls who put on skates and team jerseys today have a little girl named Abby Hoffman to thank for the fun they have on the ice!

THE GOLDEN GOAL

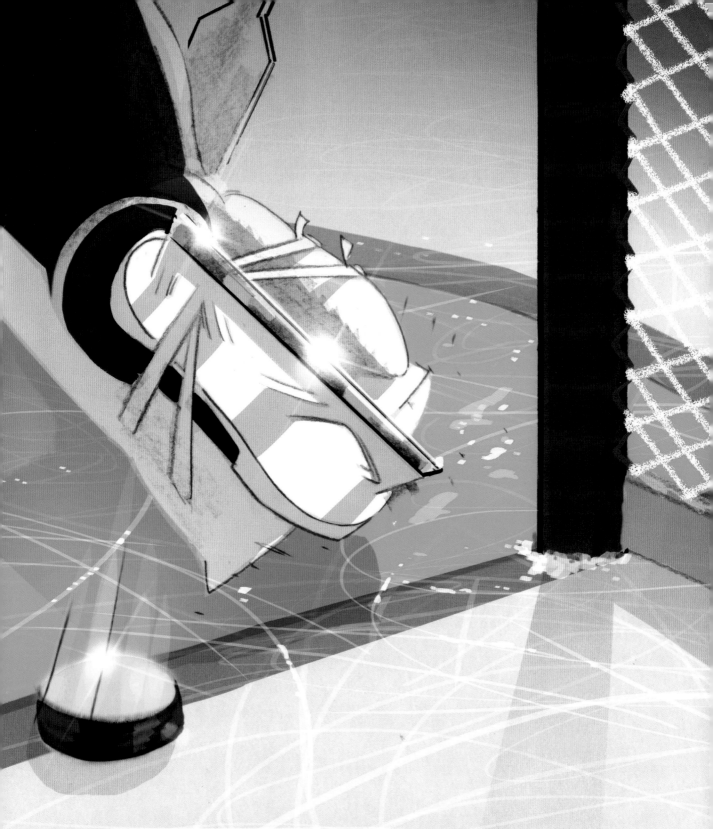

All goals are wonderful for the fans of the scoring team. All goals are reasons to celebrate. But sometimes a goal is extra special. Sometimes a goal earns the right to be called "golden."

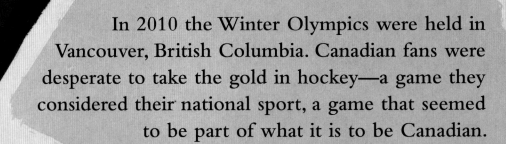

In 2010 the Winter Olympics were held in Vancouver, British Columbia. Canadian fans were desperate to take the gold in hockey—a game they considered their national sport, a game that seemed to be part of what it is to be Canadian.

But the fans were also nervous. After all, the Canadian men were playing the United States, a team they had lost to just the week before. And the Canadian team hadn't even made it to the medal round in the last Olympics. What's more, they were feeling pressure to perform well on home ice.

When the game started, both teams were playing cautiously. They didn't want to get any penalties. They didn't want to do anything that might give the other team a chance to score. But they were also playing very hard. The game was faster and more intense than even a Stanley Cup Final game.

In the first period, Canada scored a goal. The fans relaxed a little. But the players didn't.

In fact, the second period was so hard fought, with the plays moving so quickly from end to end, that some have called it one of the best periods of hockey ever played. Canada scored a second goal, but then the U.S. answered with one of its own. The two teams were separated by only one goal. Everyone in the arena and at home was on the edge of their seats.

In the third period, the Canadians took a shot, but it dinged off the goal post. And then the same thing happened with a second shot. A third shot on goal failed to make it past the goalie. Then Sidney Crosby had a breakaway—but he missed. The crowd let out a big groan. Nothing was working for the Canadians.

The last few minutes were tense. With a minute and a half left, the U.S. pulled their goalie and put on an extra player. But all Canada had to do was hold the U.S. off for ninety seconds, and they would win.

Then disaster struck.

With just 24.4 seconds to play in
the third period, U.S. player Zach Parise
grabbed a rebound and shot it into the
Canadian net. The tying goal!

Parise was so happy that
he skated straight to the boards
and jumped up to celebrate.
The arena fell silent.

The Canadian fans were stunned.
Regulation time was over. The game would be decided in overtime.

0:00
INTERMISSION
2   2

The Canadian team retreated glumly to the dressing room. The Zamboni drove out onto the ice. The fans in the stands were anxious and restless.

Head coach Mike Babcock addressed the players in the locker room. "Who's going to be our hero?" he asked.

When the game started again, the players flew back and forth across the ice.

111

Then, at seven minutes and forty seconds into overtime, Canadian Sidney Crosby and an American player skated into the boards in the U.S. end, digging after the puck. Crosby got his stick on it and sent it over to the corner, to his teammate Jarome Iginla. As Iginla battled U.S. player Ryan Suter for control, he heard, "Iggy! Iggy!"

Crosby had skated toward the net and wanted Iginla to pass the puck back to him. Iginla wrestled the puck away from his opponent and snapped it over to Crosby, falling to the ice once the puck was released. Crosby was a couple of metres to the side of the net and barely in front of it. It looked like an impossible angle.

But in the blink of an eye, Crosby snapped his stick. A low, hard shot flashed through the crease and went skidding between the goalie's pads.

Canada had won!

Crosby would later tell people that he didn't see the puck go in the net, but he knew he had scored by the roar of the crowd. The arena shook and rumbled with the happy shouts and cries of the Canadian fans.

Crosby threw his stick and gloves up in the air and was immediately surrounded by his joyful teammates.

The fans in the arena continued to go crazy. Out of their seats, cheering and shouting, some began to throw hats and other things on the ice.

Someone threw a flag attached to a huge flagpole right over the glass. Crosby skated away from the big cluster of jumping, hugging Canadian players and went over to pick up the flag. He glided around the ice with it waving behind him.

It was a moment that no one watching would ever forget.

THE GAME THAT JUST WOULDN'T END

A lot of people say that hockey is the fastest team sport there is. The skaters certainly fly across the ice. And sure, the action doesn't stop for long. But there was at least one game when hockey didn't seem very fast. And that was the game that just wouldn't end.

The longest game ever played in the NHL happened on March 24, 1936, at the Montreal Forum. The Montreal Maroons (a team that doesn't exist anymore) and the Detroit Red Wings were playing the first game in a best-of-five semifinal playoff series. After three periods, the game was tied: 0–0. After a short intermission, the first twenty-minute overtime period started. That overtime period ended in a tie.

As did the next.

And the next.

And the next.

And the next.

And the next.

In case you've lost track, that's *six* overtime periods! When the game was over, the two teams had played about as long as it takes to play three full games!

The game, which started at 8:30 at night, finished almost six hours later, at 2:25 in the morning. In other words, it started one day and finished the next!

Playing hockey for six hours would exhaust anyone, but as the game went on, it actually got harder and harder for the players. You see, the longer the game wore on, the more difficult it was to skate.

The ice surface became covered with deep scratches and holes. Skating across the rough, bumpy surface was tough work. And the puck bounced around whenever the players tried to stickhandle it along the ice.

The players' legs were so sore that, during intermissions, they lay on the benches with their feet in the air to keep the blood flowing. They also drank tea and coffee, trying to get a little pick-me-up. The two referees, who usually took their skates off between periods, stopped doing that. Their feet were getting swollen, and they were afraid they wouldn't get their skates back on.

Sure, the players and refs were having a tough time, but it's not as if the goalies had it any easier. In those days, the teams didn't use backup goalies. The two opposing goalies had to play the whole game without any breaks.

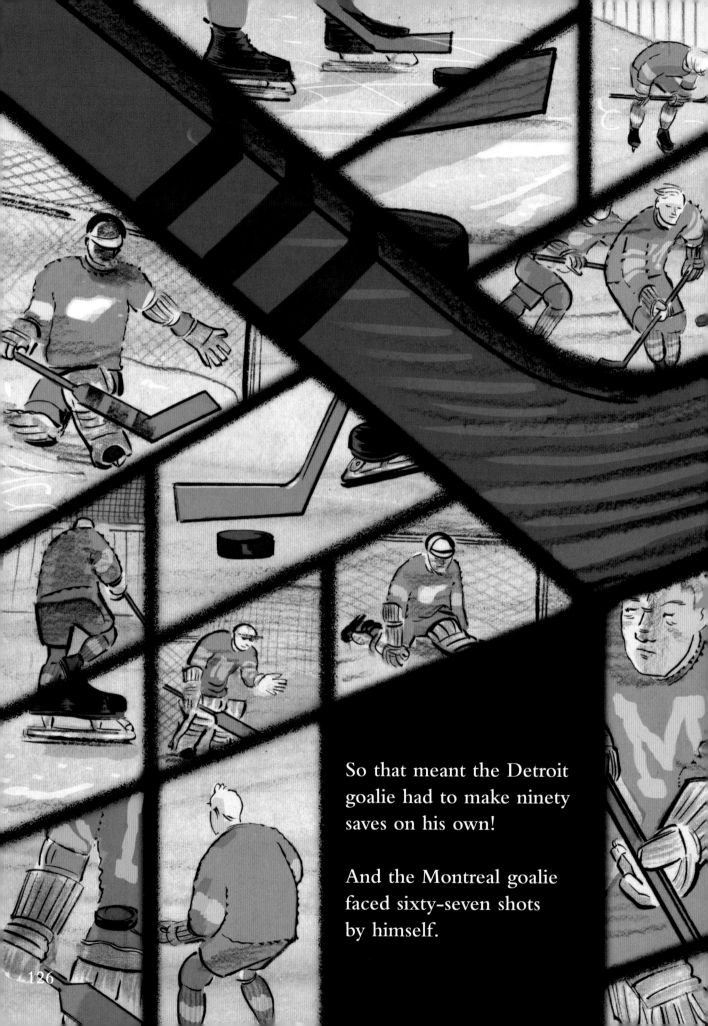

So that meant the Detroit goalie had to make ninety saves on his own!

And the Montreal goalie faced sixty-seven shots by himself.

In fact, by the end of the game, Detroit's goalie had worked so hard that he lost twelve pounds in sweat. And the equipment he wore soaked up every pound of it. His leather gloves were drenched. The horsehair stuffing in his goalie pads was wet through. His wool sweater was sodden, and his long underwear was dripping.

Now, if you watched six hours of TV, you'd be dry but probably pretty tired. Well, so were the fans watching the game at the Forum. By the time the two teams were into the later overtime periods, some of the people in the stands—those who hadn't left already, that is—were curling up on the seats and going to sleep.

In the wee hours of the morning, not too long before a lot of people in Montreal had to get up to start their day, Detroit finally scored the only goal of the game, beating the Maroons 1–0.

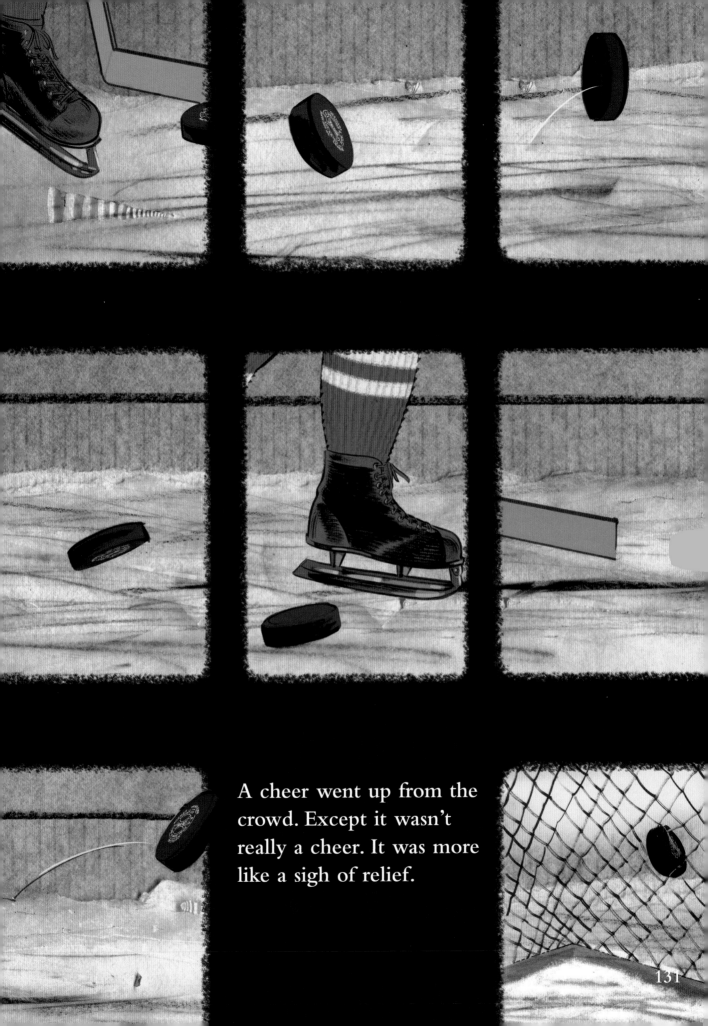

A cheer went up from the crowd. Except it wasn't really a cheer. It was more like a sigh of relief.

The NHL has long since changed the rules about overtime, so we will never see a game this long again. As much as you might love hockey, would you want to sit through a six-hour game?

133

ZAMBONI TO THE RESCUE

Hockey fans may disagree about who is the best player in the NHL or which team deserves the Stanley Cup, but there's one star of the game that everyone loves to watch on the ice: the Zamboni machine!

Believe it or not, the Zamboni wasn't invented because of hockey. It wasn't even invented in Canada. The Zamboni was born in hot and sunny California, in a little town called Paramount.

In the 1930s, Frank Zamboni had a business in Paramount that made blocks of ice for people to use to keep their food cold. But once the household refrigerator was invented, Frank needed to find a new way to use all his ice-making equipment.

So in 1940, he built himself—and the town—a big ice-skating rink, which he called Iceland. But he discovered that taking care of the ice was a big hassle.

People used to fix bumpy, chewed-up ice on skating rinks by scraping it down with shovels.

After the ice was scraped, it would be flooded with water.

All of this was done by hand. And it took at least six people and about an hour and a half to finish. Frank Zamboni could resurface his ice only once a day.

Frank decided to build a machine that would do all the refinishing steps at the same time. It was a big challenge. He built machine after machine, tinkering, adjusting, and improving. But he finally did it. And everyone who had an ice-skating rink, including all of the NHL teams, loved his new invention.

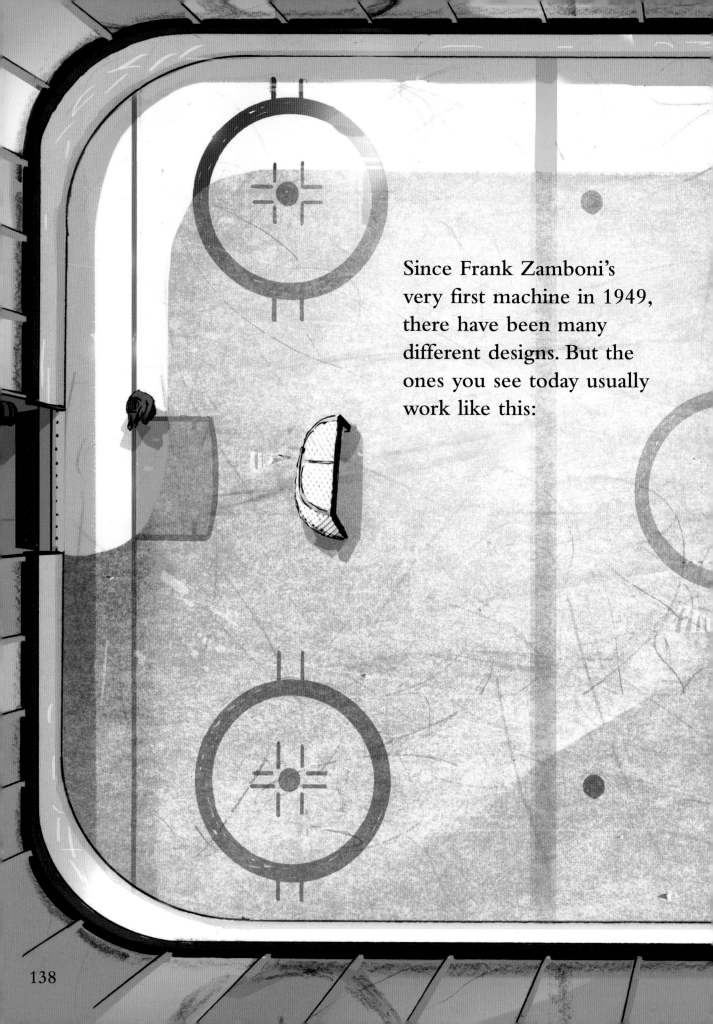

Since Frank Zamboni's very first machine in 1949, there have been many different designs. But the ones you see today usually work like this:

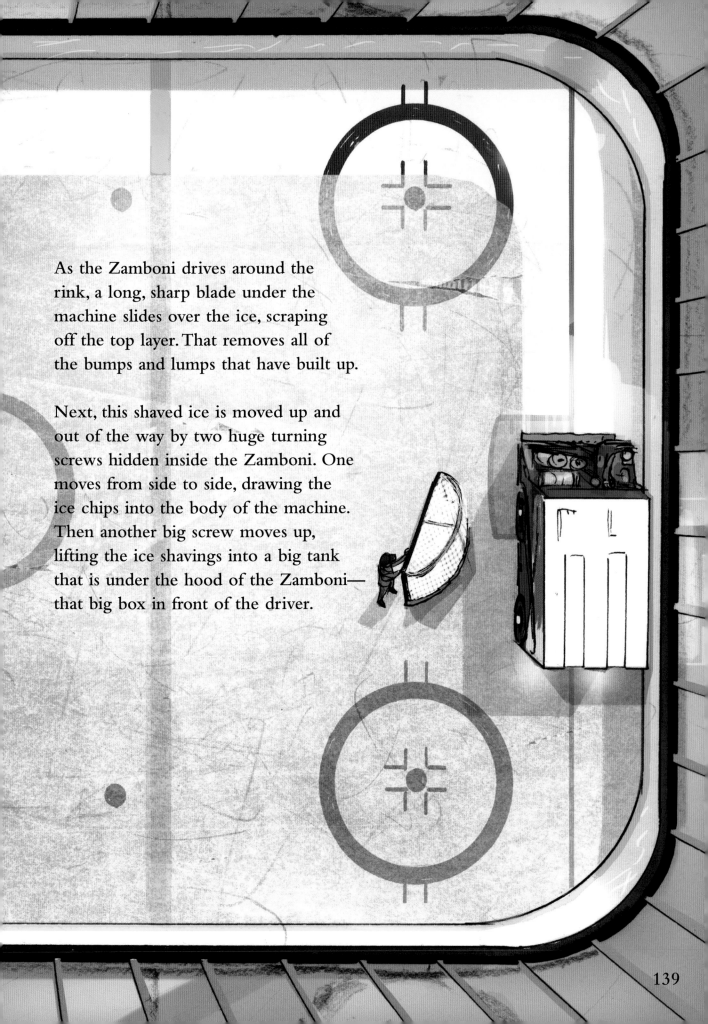

As the Zamboni drives around the
rink, a long, sharp blade under the
machine slides over the ice, scraping
off the top layer. That removes all of
the bumps and lumps that have built up.

Next, this shaved ice is moved up and
out of the way by two huge turning
screws hidden inside the Zamboni. One
moves from side to side, drawing the
ice chips into the body of the machine.
Then another big screw moves up,
lifting the ice shavings into a big tank
that is under the hood of the Zamboni—
that big box in front of the driver.

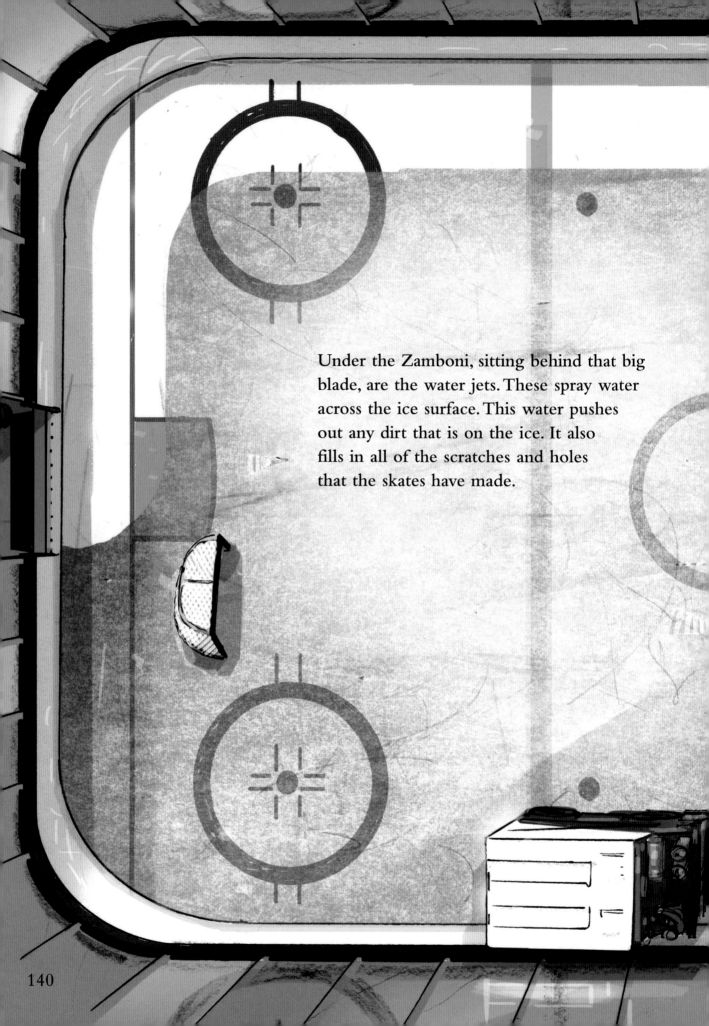

Under the Zamboni, sitting behind that big blade, are the water jets. These spray water across the ice surface. This water pushes out any dirt that is on the ice. It also fills in all of the scratches and holes that the skates have made.

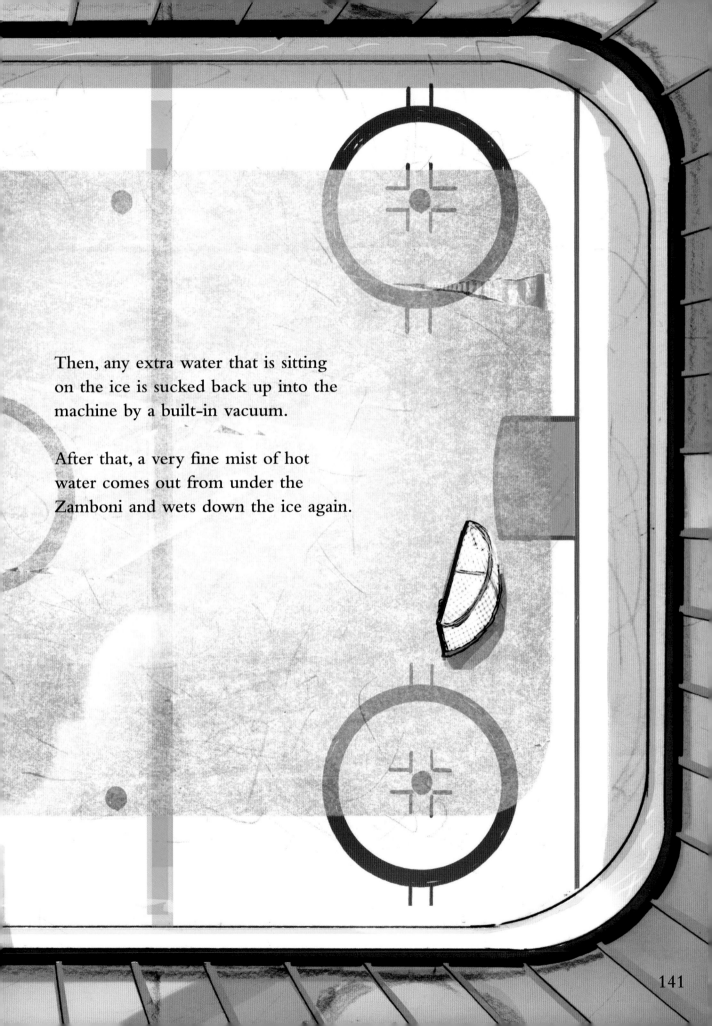

Then, any extra water that is sitting on the ice is sucked back up into the machine by a built-in vacuum.

After that, a very fine mist of hot water comes out from under the Zamboni and wets down the ice again.

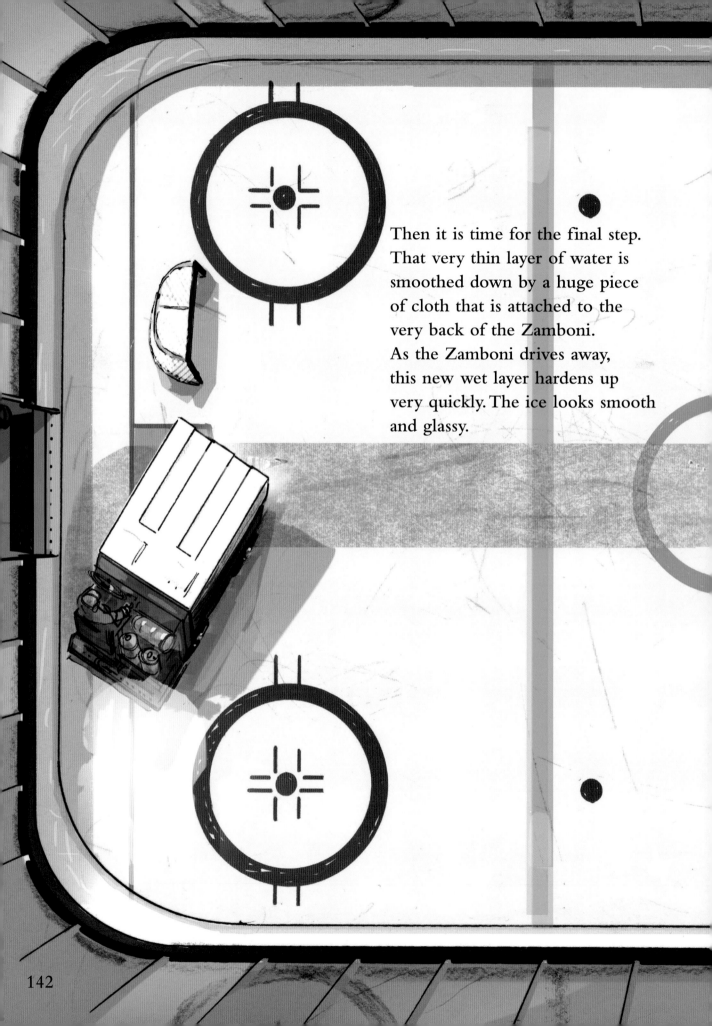

Then it is time for the final step. That very thin layer of water is smoothed down by a huge piece of cloth that is attached to the very back of the Zamboni. As the Zamboni drives away, this new wet layer hardens up very quickly. The ice looks smooth and glassy.

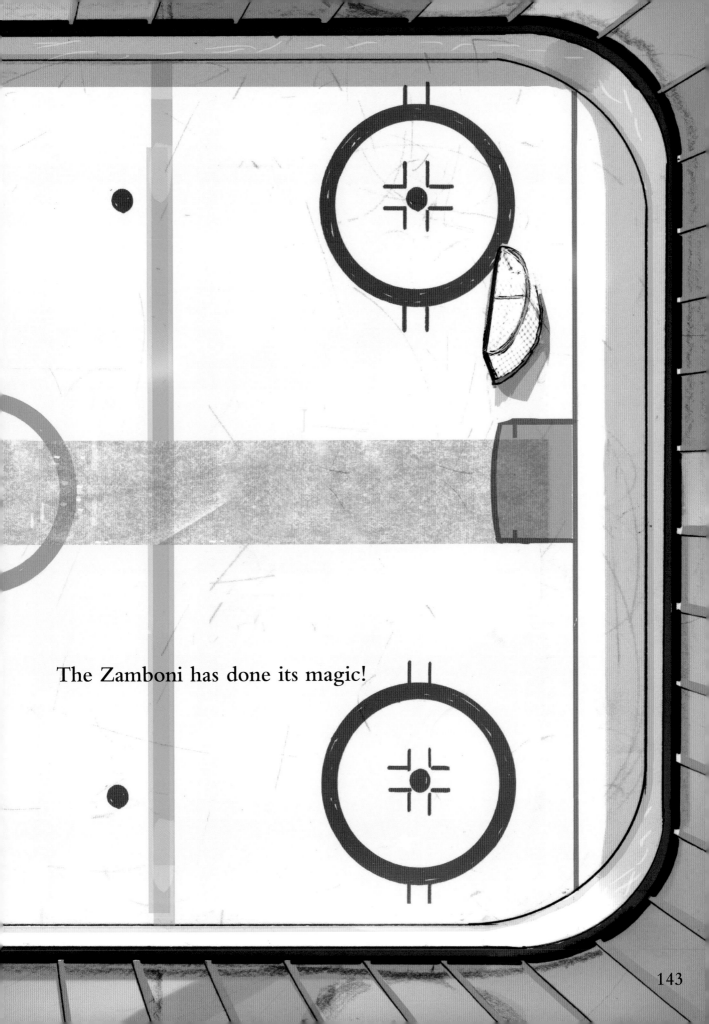

The Zamboni has done its magic!

Then the Zamboni drives outside, where the big tank in the front is emptied—leaving a huge pile of snow. When the Zamboni is finished scraping down the average ice rink, it has produced enough shaved ice to make over 3,500 snow cones!

Of course, over the years, other people
have built and sold ice-resurfacing
machines. But hockey fans know
there is nothing like Frank Zamboni's
incredible invention.

A
BIG
CREASE
TO FILL

When Carey Price was a young boy growing up in tiny Anahim Lake, British Columbia, his hockey hero was Montreal Canadiens goalie Patrick Roy. Roy is certainly one of the greatest goalies of all time. Over the course of his playing days, Roy won the Stanley Cup four times. No wonder Carey loved him!

So young Carey worked hard at becoming a good goalie. His father, who had also played goal, taught him how to block shots on the frozen creek outside their log cabin home.

When Carey wanted to play league hockey, he and his dad drove four hours to the closest town that had an indoor rink. Carey's dad even bought a plane so he could fly young Carey to his games and practices.

As he got older, Carey moved away from home to play junior and minor league hockey. In 2005, when he was not quite eighteen, he was drafted into the NHL.

And the team that picked him up? The Montreal Canadiens! Carey Price would be playing on the same team his hockey idol, Patrick Roy, had played for.

Carey had a pretty big crease to fill! And Patrick Roy wasn't the only great goalie who had stood in that net before Carey. In fact, Montreal has been home to some of hockey's best netminders: goalies such as Jacques Plante, Ken Dryden, and Georges Vezina, for whom the goalie trophy was named.

But there was something else that made playing for Montreal really challenging for any rookie on the team. You see, Montreal is a city that really, really loves its hockey. And it has a long, long history with the game.

In the early days of the NHL, Montreal actually had two NHL teams—the Montreal Maroons and the Montreal Canadiens. The city is so passionate about hockey, in fact, that fans often boo their own team and players if they are not living up to expectations! There was no doubt about it—it was going to be pretty tough for young Carey Price to win over the Montreal fans.

Carey Price's first game for the Montreal Canadiens was on October 10, 2007. It was exactly twenty-two years after Patrick Roy had played his first full game in the Canadiens' net! And if that wasn't coincidence enough, Montreal was facing the Pittsburgh Penguins, just as they had been when Roy made his debut. In Roy's first game he allowed only three goals. The Penguins goalie let in five. Montreal won the game. Would Price be able to live up to his idol's performance?

Price was excited when he stepped out onto the ice.

It's a good thing Price didn't fluster easily. In the first period, the Canadiens got a number of penalties. That meant Price had to face several power plays. With more men on the ice, the Penguins descended on the Canadiens' net, shooting puck after puck.

Price managed to block them all!

In the second period, the Penguins got a shot past Price on another power play. In the third period, the Penguins brought a puck from behind the net to score. But Montreal scored three times, which was enough to win. Carey Price played an even better debut game than his hero.

After the victory, almost everyone agreed that young Price had won the game for them. The newbie had turned away shot after shot after shot. He made twenty-six saves in total, including a couple of pucks hit by another incredible young player— Sidney Crosby.

Although it started off really well, Price's first year did have a few bumps. He was sent back down to the minors for a while, but when he came back he was stronger than ever. By the end of the regular season, he was Montreal's starting goaltender and had a better record than any other rookie goaltender in the league.

As each year went by, over and over again Carey Price proved himself worthy of standing in the Canadiens' net. In 2014, he was between the posts as the Canadian men's team won Olympic gold.

And in 2015, he had such a spectacular
year that he won four trophies:
the Jennings, the Vezina, the Hart,
and the Ted Lindsay. He was the first
player in NHL history to win all four
in one season!

Just like his hero, Patrick Roy, Carey
Price is now considered one of the
best goalies on the globe.

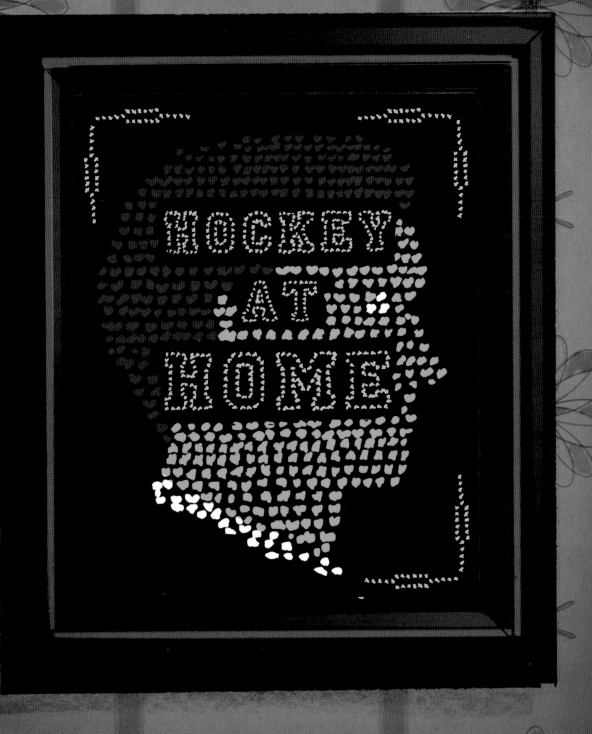

Mario Lemieux is a big hockey star. He played for the Pittsburgh Penguins and then became the team's owner. And if you asked him who helped him become such a great player, he would no doubt talk about Maman and Papa—his mom and dad. He might tell you that, with their help, he actually learned to play hockey in his childhood living room!

And no, Mario doesn't mean mini-sticks, or table hockey, or even watching hockey on TV. What he is talking about is much stranger—and much more magical.

Mario's family loved hockey. Each and every one of them. Papa. The boys, Alain, Richard, and Mario.

And maybe most of all,

Maman.

Papa had built the boys a rink on the front lawn so they could practise skating and learn hockey. They played on it whenever they could.

But one day the snow was coming down so hard that the rink was completely buried. Papa shovelled off the ice, but the snow kept coming. It snowed and it snowed and it snowed. The boys were outside in their boots trying to help their father, but they couldn't keep up. The snow was up to little Mario's waist. Finally, the boys and their father decided to give up and go inside.

The boys threw the front door open and marched into the house. Before the door closed, a gust of wind blew in a white cloud of snow. Alain, Richard, and Mario headed right to the living room to tell their mother about all the snow and the shovelling.

They were covered head to toe in the white stuff. As they stood on the carpet, it fell off their boots and off their legs. Chunks slid off their hats and the ends of their mittens.

171

"Stop, stop," said Maman. "Look at my carpet!"

The boys dropped their eyes to the floor. The rug was covered in big white lumps that were beginning to melt, spreading dark circles across the wool. But the boys were too disappointed about the rink to care about the carpet. They were upset that they couldn't play their favourite game. Maman looked at their sad faces, and then she looked at the snow-covered carpet. She placed her slippered foot on a patch of snow. She stomped the snow down until it was hard and slippery.

"I have an idea," Maman announced. "But I'll need your help."

The first thing Maman did was walk over to the thermostat. She snapped it off. "No heat this evening," she said.

Then she got the boys and Papa to open all the windows downstairs. Great gusts of ice crystals filled the house.

"We have to get this place good and cold," she said.

Next, she threw open the front door. "And now for the snow!"

173

Then Maman walked outside. She came back in a few seconds later with a shovel piled high with white fluff. She carried it over to the living room and dumped it right in the middle of the carpet! The boys could not believe it. She went back outside and came in again with another shovelful of snow. In and out. In and out. Each time she brought more snow.

Before long, the carpet had completely disappeared under a blanket of sparkling white. After tipping the final shovelful of snow onto the carpet, Maman put the shovel on the floor and leaned against it. She looked around. The living room was getting very cold now. The boys could even see their breath.

Then Maman picked up the shovel again. She began to walk all over the hidden carpet, smacking the wet snow down until it was hard and even.

When she was done, the snow had frozen into a flat sheet of silver ice, shiny and slippery. The living room had been turned into an indoor skating rink!

Maman turned to the boys.

"Voila," she said. "Get your skates on!"

As the snow continued to fall outside, Alain, Richard,
and Mario played hockey in their living room.

They skated past the sofa. They moved the puck around the table legs.
They checked each other in front of the TV. The overhead light twinkled,
and the photos on the walls stared down at them in wonder.

Later Maman would tell people, "They really did quite a job on my rug." Not everyone believed she had actually turned her living room into a hockey rink and let her little hockey players ruin the carpet. But that's the way hockey star Mario Lemieux remembers it—a frozen carpet, an icy living room, and the coziest, homiest hockey rink ever.